ANTIQUE
Dreams

The Diary of an Old Lady in Love

BY
JERRI BRILLHART

First published by Interdimensional Press
February 2019

ISBN: 9780991197057

Library of Congress Control Number: 2019930466

Printed in the United States of America

This book is printed on Acid free paper

To My Mother

Acknowledgments

I wish to thank all my friends and family for their love and support during my 101-year journey on Planet Earth, especially my daughters, Suzanne, Marsha, and Marilyn. A special thanks to my grandson, John Lund, who designed and produced the cover artwork. I love you with all my heart.

I also wish to thank my dear friend Ginny Burns, who volunteered as my editor on this book as well as my first book, "My 100 Years In the Rhythm & Flow," published on my 100th birthday, September 23, 2017.

I am also grateful to Don Huntington for his beautifully written Foreword, and to my publishers, Pat and Byron McCulley of Interdimensional Press in Brentwood, California. And to all my friends at Brentwood Unity, I love you all!

Foreword

Jerri Brillhart possesses a character like a finely-polished gemstone. The sparkle in her eye, the smile on her lips, the words of comfort, encouragement, or inspiration for others result from Jerri's having spent more than a century being tumbled about in life's polishing machine.

Through innumerable victories and defeats during the past 101 years, Jerri has used the power of her imagination to fire her soul with courage and hope to deny power to any toxic person or threatening circumstance. As a result, she's become a beautiful gem in the hand of God and in the eyes of the people who know and love her.

Ever since I first met her five years ago in our little church, Jerri has continually captivated me with her cheerful witticisms, sage philosophies, and creative approaches toward life. Occasionally, she will stand before our congregation on Sunday morning and read a pithy poetic commentary on some aspect of life. One Sunday, Jerri read a poem that in 40 words seemed to capture the life-long perspective that led to her becoming such a compelling and beautiful soul:

We all possess within our hearts
The gift of imagination.
As we discover and use it,
We find we can create

Our very own happiness, or
Bring ourselves unhappiness.
Every day we use our imagination
To enrich or destroy ourselves.

In the following pages, pay close attention to Jerri's words and the example of her life. Learn to see the world as Jerri sees it -- to understand that life continually reveals lovely gifts that will be obscured if you remain mired in negative attitudes and beliefs.

Your own liberated imagination can free you from fear, disappointment, and resentment simply by learning to look -- as Jerri always looks -- for a root of good in every person, a positive quality in every circumstance, and a hopeful response to every challenge. In that way you will allow people and events to polish your lives and give you a Jerri-like sparkle and glow. As you read this book, may God give you the energy and intention to allow that to happen.

— Dr. Don Huntington
Editorial Director
110 Magazine
Brentwood, California

My First Love

In the Spring of my 17th year, I was living with my family in Chicago when destiny introduced me to the love of my life. Rollin was two years older than I and he quickly became the center of my life.

My friend Ione was dating Rollin's friend Ed, so she arranged a double date for the four of us. Romance was in the air, and by the end of the date Rollin was my boyfriend.

Cupid's arrow stuck us good. Our lives became divided between blissful hours together and restless days apart. Rollin's work allowed little time for those "blissful hours" that both of us longed for. He was a proofreader on the swing shift for *Esquire Magazine,* leaving weekends as the only time for romance.

But I couldn't complain. We were in the midst of the Great Depression and Rollin was lucky to have a job. There was no way he could afford an automobile, so we often walked around Chicago's South Side or rode streetcars in the famous "Loop." We attended summer concerts in Grant Park and silent films or vaudeville shows on State Street. Rollin bought me fragrant gardenias at the flower stands along the "L" and spicy ethnic dishes that we ate on street corners.

Rollin always paid for everything. For one thing, he had a job so he was actually making some money. In those days, a gentleman never permitted a lady to pay for anything, so I smiled and said *"thank you"*. In those days, I assumed it was appropriate to get a free ride at my boyfriend's expense. It's what everyone thought because this was decades before women's liberation.

One summer we learned to play tennis, or at least we tried. The only thing I can remember about the sport is that the scoring had something to do with *Love*, as did all our other activities that summer.

We continued our romance through the heat and humidity of August and into the winter blizzards that periodically brought transportation to a grinding halt. The winds whipped between the buildings as "The Windy City" made every effort to live up to its name. Perfectly heedless of whatever was happening with the weather, Rollin and I continued our long walks through the city, excursions interrupted only by periods of delicious cuddling.

The flames of love were burning hot, so each weekend we spent as much time as possible in each other's company, burning the candle at both ends. We were unable to say goodnight after those blissful Saturdays together, and the morning sunshine would usually find us still together.

Social norms were different in those days, which meant the approaching daylight found me in his company and sometimes in his arms, but never in his bed. Rollin and I never took advantage of the other's sweet innocence but found ways of making our own discoveries about the birds and the bees.

On Sunday evenings, Rollin would go back to his swing shift with almost no sleep during the previous 36 or sometimes 48 hours. It was remarkable that he managed to do that week after week without collapsing from exhaustion.

Beginning with that first double-date, the two of us were in an exclusive relationship. I wore his class ring as a symbol of the unspoken bond between us, but we were so impoverished that there was no talk of marriage.

When my family moved to California, I had to say goodbye to Rollin. It was like leaving a part of me behind in Illinois. Someone told me that "absence makes the heart grow fonder," but the truth is that absence is to love as wind is to a flame -- it extinguishes the small and enkindles the great.

For a time, Rollin's love for me remained strong. This was three decades before affordable long-distance phone calls and five decades before email, so Rollin had to maintain assurances of his continued affection by a stream of special delivery letters.

There was a brief time of hopefulness when he came to California to try to get employment. However, the Depression was in full swing, there were no jobs, and he was forced to return to his proofreading job in Illinois, while I remained in sunny California to establish my career as a secretary.

One day the letters ceased to come. The end didn't arrive as a tragedy but rather as a poignant reminder that some romances endure only as a lovely memory.

Now that I am an old lady, it seems to me that so many of us deny our true feelings and allow ourselves to be swayed by outside circumstances. We are so conditioned by religious creeds that say, "It is more blessed to give than to receive," that we forget we are inherently lovable -- not only by giving to others but by being our true selves. Too many times I have neglected to embrace the joy that marked my time with Rollin because I ignored the promptings of my heart.

One of the most precious qualities a person of my advanced age can have is hopefulness. That happened when I learned that Rollin was planning a trip to California with the intention of staking his claim on me again. Both our spouses had died within six months of each other and he thought we could rekindle our long lost love and end our days together.

The following is a poetic journal of my "second time around" love affair with Rollin, over 50 years later.

June 25, 1989

My old "Beau" from the 1930s
Telephoned last Saturday night,
Immediately spanning space and time
And old anxieties.
We talked about the good old days,
Recalling some moments we had shared,
Along with, "And do you remember him?"
Or, "Did you hear that she had died?"
The phone bill kept ticking on,
But we didn't care for we were
Both lonely and needed to touch
With voice and heart those yesteryears
When we were young and so full of hope,
Exploring the universe and its delights.
But now that age has captured us
In different bodies and places,
We reach out by telephone
To snatch the bygone days.

September 25, 1989

While I sat draped in a flimsy bed sheet
After my soothing body massage,
His soft, friendly, sexy voice came
On so strong while he safely
Lounged some 2,000 miles away.
In the course of our long conversation,
His questions undressed me while he
Explored my weight, my height,
My blood pressure, as well as
My vitamin intake.
On and on he talked and pried
As if knowing my body
Was very vulnerable.
But distance is a wonderful ally,
A comfort when you feel threatened.
Well, he can "make believe" and still
Feel secure holding his telephone
Receiver instead of me.

September 26, 1989

Your voice and tone and laughter
Keep returning to my mind.
Is it the power of suggestion
Or a hypnotizing web
That entangles my
Subconscious with your aura?
I close you off with daily tasks
But somehow you sneak in,
Upsetting all my well-planned
Goals of unencumbered freedom.
Do I need you, want you or
Even care about you?
Or is it just a replay
Of a long ago romance?

September 27, 1989

Distance has some advantages,
At least in physical ways.
But when it comes to emotions
The miles just melt away.
For it is in the mind
That the bond occurs
With words and attitudes
Expressed between the lines.
You have slipped into my heart
When I was unaware,
Stealing my natural defenses
Like walls I've hidden there.
So please, don't telephone again
Unless I know you are a man
Of honorable intentions.

September 28, 1989

Voices and silent vibrations
Create a web of feelings that could
Bind me in spite of 2,000 miles.
If I never answered the phone
We could not continue this game,
For sooner or later
A platonic status evolves
Into a trap.
I've been tied by vows before
That chained me to tradition,
So now that I have broken free
Why don't you please
Let me go to pasture?

October 3, 1989

He was my first love
Long, long ago.
He quickened my heart,
My body, my soul.
With his gentle ministrations
And soothing ways, he healed
My turbulence as I was
Stepping into womanhood.
After 50 years of separation
There was always a tiny place where
I kept wondering how he was.
Through time and space
My antennae kept alive
My curiosity about him.
Recently we each completed
Long marriages with others and
When the doors were safely closed
We opened up the attic of our youth,
Finding antique dreams
That were still intact
In both of us.

Look out Virgo

Libra snatches ideas from the air,
Scrutinizing, analyzing, summarizing and
Materializing in fascinating ways.
So look out Virgo, caught in neatness,
You are about to be shaken,
Sparked and invigorated by ideas
That disrupt your well-planned Earth,
Filling you with lots of mirth.
Are you ready for these changes
That intrude upon your quiet nest?
What will happen to your teacups
When they're tossed from shelves
And you find yourself in pieces,
Needing to be re-glued
Into some new creation
For a fuller life?
Are you willing to let go and fly
Into another dream, or
Will you be a fuddy-duddy,
Scared to death
To live again?

October 4, 1989

In Virgo's offhand way
About such delicate feelings,
He said, "*Will you be my girlfriend*?"
I couldn't see his eyes or
Earnest look, as he dropped
His words into the phone.
Not seeing with my eyes,
But feeling with my heart,
He touched a vulnerable spot,
Desperately reaching
Across the miles
In the same shy way
I remembered him
Some 50 years ago
When he was my
Sweet young beau.

October 5, 1989

While I am in the
Autumn of my life
The many parts of me
Are slowly changing.
I shall savor this fall
Season, knowing that
It is my last fling,
As desire for adventure
Brings me through
Many changes into
Another kind of Spring
With you.

October 7, 1989

I am scheming of how the furniture
Should be placed and how the shades
Should be drawn and how the walls
Must be changed for his contentment.
I am getting the nest ready
For the gentle snow bird
To come south this winter
And bask in my sun.
I wonder if it will
Be too hot for him?
His heart may be thawing
But his feet may be lead;
I wonder if I can shake him up
So he will dance with me again?

October 8, 1989

When our hearts are depressed
With grieving and our bodies
Don't want to move
We need to be helped
To our feet by a friend
Who knows just what to do.
Like a car that can't run
When its battery is dead
Or the cash register fails
At the supermarket stand,
Or the plane can't fly
When the clouds are too low,
God sends us a friend to
Brighten the day and give
Us strength and persistence
To push off the heavy load.

October 10, 1989

Last night he called again to check
Upon the flowers in my garden.
What variety grew in California?
He talked about the fragrant peonies
That spring out and fill
The summer air in Illinois.
The lavender of lilacs
Were thoroughly discussed.
Oh, earthy Virgo, planted in the soil,
He's really not a total bore
As he talks of earth and hearth.
A Homing Pigeon of sorts,
That I am very sure.
He really wanted to touch some
Part of me with his words but
His tongue and heart were tied.
He was out of practice on that score.
He gets ten points from me for
At least making the call.

Monday Night Call

At 9 p.m. the telephone rang.
Now this was Monday night.
I had not answered it on Sunday
Because some part of me
Was not up to listening then.
I had heard his ring last night
But just played hard to get.
He never leaves messages on
My answering machine --
He has his own peculiar reasons.
So at last I picked up the ringing
Phone and he started
Conversing just like before.
Nothing romantic did he utter;
He could have been talking
To his very own mother.
I could not insert a "sweetie"
Or a "dearie" for fear he might
Have an acute heart attack.
I just had to let him lead the
Conversation about trees, flowers,
The changes of heat and humidity,
When I kept wishing
He would simply say,
"I love you."

October 15, 1989

Thoughts of you
Absorb my time
While I imagine
Affectionate adventures
Arousing us
With astonishment.
We may be breathless,
But we shall remain calm,
Delighted by our eagerness
To be electrified, grateful
For the turn of events
That inspire us to be loving
Toward each other again.
We relax in this wonderful
Sensitive situation, and trust
That tenderness will touch
Our hearts with warmth
When we meet again.

October 17, 1989

I often wonder
"What does an old woman
Want of a man these days?"
It can't be just monetary security,
But sometimes that can be so.
Perhaps she needs his presence
For comfort in her golden years.
Gentle old loving men are a rarity,
Getting to be endangered species
Disappearing from this earth
Like certain plants and trees.
Lonely old women are left to settle
Into clusters among themselves,
A constant reminder of how life
Moves men into the Great Hereafter.
So when a second chance romance
Falls into your lap,
You better sit up
And take notice.

The Adrenalin Zoom

He is stirring me with phone calls,
Making my heart really sing.
He is getting out of his shell
Just thinking of me again.
There is nothing like being in love
That makes the blood flow
And the adrenalin zoom.
And when he starts to twinkle
His chuckle melts my heart.
Oh, if I'm only dreaming and
This really isn't true,
Please let me rest
A little longer so I can
Catch my breath
While meditating
Over you.

October 18, 1989

This morning I woke up early,
Crying with happiness --
A silly womanly thing to do.
Aware of what's happening
In the secret parts of me,
Like a school girl in love,
Feeling wild and carefree.
Last night when you said,
"How are you, honey?"
I really heard you then --
My heart kept recording
Your simple refrain,
"I love you."

October 21, 1989

Mr. Perfection is getting himself
Spruced up from top to toe.
Ordering new glasses
So he can really see me,
Going through the doctor's
Extensive physical exams
So he can pass the crucial test
Of holding my hand and
Whatever else he plans.
I have tried to reassure him
In a thousand different ways
That I will give him space,
But what he really wants,
Is just to hold me close,
Letting me know
He really loves me
Just as he did
So very long ago.

October 22, 1989

My old beau is wooing me
Again by telephone.
He is lonesome for a woman's touch,
A woman's heart and her romance.
He is getting heated up
With dreams and making plans
To get from where he is
To where he'll find me.
I wonder if he will come by train
Or plane, or take a Greyhound bus?
Perhaps he will be a passenger
In someone else's shiny Jaguar.
But then again he may purchase
A slick new Toyota.
Will he arrive all out of breath,
Hugging me so tight he breaks a rib?
Or will he brush his lips upon my cheek
Like any old ordinary brother?
I'll love whichever way he comes,
By train or plane or bus, but
Why is he so slow
In making up his mind
To get here?

October 24, 1989

Oh, I wish you were here beside me,
Just holding my hand in yours
Like you once did long, long ago
While we rode the leaping "L"
Or huddled on the top step,
Being romantic in the wee hours,
Or mesmerized by dim-lit shows
Of Old Chicago...
Despite the passing years,
With paths of different directions,
There still remained in my mind
Some special memories of you,
Tucked away in my heart
Where once in a while I would peek,
Getting in touch with you again.
Though we were miles apart
You were always there
As close as my heart.
Destiny brought us together
After 50 years of separation,
So now we can share a dream,
Both going together
In the same direction.

November 1, 1989

We are beginning negotiations
Of how he will place his funds
For his romantic winter interlude;
How he will arrange for a house sitter
To protect and care for his homestead
While he leaves the chilly winds
For California's brilliant sun.
He is rearranging his thinking and
His life is getting in touch
With pent-up feelings
He never knew he had.
He agrees to rearrange his values,
Bringing them into modern times,
Examining his needs and recognizing
The strange stirrings that propel him
Forward into a kind of transformation.
We sit on the brink of new beginnings,
Guided by some unseen forces to
Move together with future plans.
I suggest, and he resists, but
Then he is changing bit by bit.

November 2, 1989

The magnetic current lying within
Attracts what you believe.
As your good comes into view and
You can feel and see it happening,
Realize that your faith has made it so.
Give your subconscious mind a problem
To work on as you sleep,
Your faithful servant will supply
All the solutions by morning.
Just remember to give thanks
For your blessings and divine guidance
That moves you along your chosen path,
Knowing that you must supply
The positive beliefs that your
Silent servant will bring
To your wonderful abundant good.
Your subconscious is not limited
Except by your own limited thoughts.
So say "I can" and "I am" to
Reach your desired goals!

November 4, 1989

Yesterday the holiday red amaryllis
Arrived from Medford, Oregon --
A subtle statement that only an
Old advertising executive could dream up.
I knew it was from my old beau in Chicago
Getting inside my heart again.
The brown dead-looking bulb held
Its own secrets of an early bloom.
I couldn't help thinking of how symbolic
Was its slumbering splendor that only
Needed my tender care to quicken and
Nourish it with gentle smiles and
Coaxing manner so it could flourish,
Showing its true colors when
Its blossoming would take place.
How like our love that was slowly
Coming into view, revealing our secret too.
As I held his love offering in my hands,
It was a statement and an omen,
For there was a parallel between
This hardy amaryllis bulb that
Appeared so dormant in the autumn,
Holding within its hidden layers
The potential for its future splendor.
All that was required would be the skill
Of certain love and special nurturing
To coax its beauty into fruition.
Just like the heart he was entrusting
To me, I could sense that in due time
His heart would flower like the amaryllis.

November 5, 1989

We have so much to enjoy
When we use our minds correctly;
The simple pleasure of stretching
A moment or two at a time,
Remembering a long ago romance,
Her laughter or his raised eyebrows
At a surprise event long past.
The moments we cherish and measure
Are the simple things in life
We recall in our leisure.
It isn't wealth we gather
That warms our hearts with delight;
It's just the simple acts of love
We share with one another --
Those moments of pleasure given
That make all the years
Such a treasure.

Moments

Let's use our lives
A moment at a time,
Savoring each golden morsel
With delight, watching
The seagull's lofty flight,
Smelling the fragrant roses
Displaying their wondrous hues;
Relishing a glorious sunrise,
Embracing a radiant moon,
Realizing that God
Has given us
Another chance to love
And bloom.

November 6, 1989

Yesterday I told him to burn his bridges,
Not realizing my subconscious message.
Then I began to ponder on what bridges
We all build within our mind and thoughts,
Creating bridges to health, happiness and joy
Or thoughts expressed with careless words
Of anxiety, fear, hate or resentment,
Building bridges that reveal a life
Of pain, disease and illness.
So analyze the bridges that your
Thoughts create to lift you up
Or let you down and
Burden you with pain.
The bridge I built, thought by thought,
Was stretched over the years with words
And feelings that served me well.
I sometimes had to destroy useless
Worn out bridges that could not
Carry me across a turbulent river,
But with my inner guide I learned
To build a bridge of strength
That stood the test of time,
Allowing me to survive.
So now that I am more mature
I'll gladly share my bridge with you.

November 10, 1989

My dear, you have a huge bank account
Awaiting your withdrawal of accumulated
Interest that has piled up since 1936.
Old memories held in that account
Are going to pay off in dividends.
So when you arrive on California soil,
Remember it's my turn to spoil.
You may have three kisses at the start,
Along with one to three hugs per day.
I'll even throw in a few "I-love-yous"
Just to brighten up your day.
Of course, while the candle burns hotly
I will sometimes wink a little coyly
Indicating by some subtle sign that
Now is the time to rendezvous.

Impulses

My love finally made a commitment
To follow through and really get here,
To hold my hand and whisper
His intentions and how he feels.
His curiosity has made him move,
Wondering if the images in his brain
Match what his subconscious is feeling,
And if all those jumbled thoughts
Will fit together like a jigsaw puzzle
As his words come tumbling out
Of his activated right and left spheres,
Bringing harmony to his impulses.

November 13, 1989

He has broken the news to his family
That he is California-bound.
His daughter-in-law's joy was unsurpassed,
Happy to learn he had a place to keep warm.
He is getting worked up to the idea that
He will hide with me from prying eyes
Our combined families may cast upon us.
My oldest daughter is asking for his address
As well as wanting to fly to Fullerton
As soon as he gets off the Amtrak.
I informed her gently, *"Hands off!"*
We need to be alone without interruptions.
We had no such complications when we were
Young sweethearts, but we have gathered
Assorted family ties in intervening years.
So please just give us time and space
To be alone together
In this newfound place.

Comparison

I have not mentioned to my stepdaughters
The love affair I am having with my old beau;
I just can't imagine what their thoughts might be
Since to them I was always their father's wife.
Now what will become of this long, strong alliance
When I step out of my neat traditional role?
Will they be glad and accepting of change or
Will they be alarmed for the safety of my brain?
Will they agree he is Mr. Wonderful, or will
They compare him with
Their dearly beloved father?

Round Trip Ticket

He has bought a round trip ticket on Amtrak,
Coming west in first class style,
Packing his duds and getting in step
To roll along the tracks of
The southern route, peeking out
Rail coach windows, curious to see
How country life and city lights
Reveal the American panorama.
He is thinking like a schoolboy
Of this momentous trip,
His blood pressure rising
As he comes to grips with his passion
For a railway trip and the idea
Of smooching with the girl
He hasn't seen in years.
I threatened to call the local newspaper
To chronicle this unusual love story but
He shuddered at the mere thought of it.
So I will dress discreetly to greet
Him at the station, wearing dark glasses
So nobody will dare suspect that I am
Acting like a young harlot.

November 14, 1989

We have had these past months
To air out our assorted thoughts.
We only had our voices
To make the vital connection
Without the static of
Face-to-face communication
With eyes, smell
Or sense of touch,
Just words that needed to be said
To clear out our attics and
Bury our anxieties among innuendos.
No body language could be read with
Expressions of silent vacant stares
Or invisible ways of draining each other
With an overkill of wasted solicitude.
We have cut through all that nonsense
With feeling words that communicated
What needed to be aired and tested.
Abstract ideas can be turned and twisted
To tease and be grossly misinterpreted,
But when you follow up the words with
Solid action, that is the real test
Of a truly significant relationship.

November 15, 1989

There is no fool like an old fool,
I have often heard repeated.
But is that really true?
It just depends on who says it.
For when the young are full of sap
They never think it foolish to
Make judgments of elder lovers.
Their perceptions are so limited
By their inexperience to view the
Interior of the seasoned heart.

A Hopeless Romantic

I must be a hopeless romantic
For at age 72 I still feel young.
However, at this marvelous stage
I have lost my inhibitions that once
Dictated a Victorian stance that
I must raise some questioning eyebrows
When my dancing legs begin to prance.
Someone once said,
"It takes a long time to become young"
And now I believe it, because I never
Was so lighthearted when I was 21.

Stoking

Now my stoic old beau is getting into
The act of dropping his negativity,
Realizing he is emerging from a
Depression he never knew he had.
He is getting into wondering
Where his life is heading,
Surmising that another 20 years
Of romance can be a possibility.
He is taking a mental calculation
Of how to preserve his aging body,
Making it really work and perk,
While his imagination seduces him
Into believing the fire just
Needs a little stoking.

A Lot of Words

Yesterday, *Roget's International Thesaurus*
Arrived from Mr. Wonderful through UPS,
Containing 256,000 words and phrases.
Now, that is certainly a lot of words
To dump on anybody's doorstep, but
I suppose he'll try making me stay home
To digest, peruse, and aptly construct
My thoughts I glibly call free verse.
Perhaps I'll slip it beneath my pillow
To be absorbed by my great subconscious,
Knowing I'll never find time
Even consciously to digest it.
He is going to have more surprises
The moment he looks into my eyes,
And finds no words to utter.

November 18, 1989

Last night when you called
I felt so close to you that
2,000 miles of separation
Just vanished into thin air.
We kind of slipped into
Each others' unseen bodies,
While my pulse raced and
Heat rose just by the
Sound of your voice.
You are quickening my spirit
And making me long for you
More and more. I don't know
Whether to cry with joy, or cry
Because I don't want to wait
Another 53 more days.

November 29, 1989

I wonder if I'm too old for modern styles
Such as romantic live-in boyfriends.
Just what's the difference between
Matrimony and shared living quarters?
Is it better to be closer or
Does it breed a kind of *laissez-faire*,
Allowing space to keep your identity
Without the benefit of clergy?
Can I pack my bag and leave anytime
My fancy dictates, thinking I am
Free to fly abroad to places like Tahiti?
Having no restraints to bind
With written codes of conduct
And decorum that strangle the Libido?
If love should be free and flowing,
Why be shackled by a marriage contract
That immediately begins to make you
What the other one believes you should be?

Light and Loving

Let's keep it light and loving,
Basking in the warmth and glow
Of light fantastic vibrations
Emanating from our inner soul.
Let's keep it joyous and free
From criticism of how I clean the house
Or don't pat you when you're down,
Or don't lift a finger when you grumble
Above the overload of dirty clothes
That clutter up the bedroom.
Let's just forget about mundane issues
Of bills, taxes and insurance premiums.
While you clip your stock dividends,
I'll tend to my checkbook and options
So we can laugh and meditate upon
Our situation of divided interests.

November 30, 1989

Oh, he did it again by sending me
365 days neatly printed and bound
That reveal the coming year.
It came by parcel post from the
National Geographic Society and
Aptly called an Engagement Calendar.
The first date I have chronicled
Is January 10, when Amtrak
Brings Mr. Wonderful to me again.
I can just imagine that I will
Recognize him immediately as
I see him searching for his luggage
Near the open track of unclaimed bags.
I hope the sun is shining brightly
As I welcome him and he hugs me
For the first time in 50 years.
Now I'm marking my calendar,
Counting days, hours and minutes,
Until he kisses me again.

December 1, 1989

Oh, by the way, how are you today?
That's how he opens the phone
Conversation these days.
He sounds so on top that I know
Some internal change has
Maneuvered him in my direction.
He is thinking up and
Getting into shape to take
Another risk with life.
He was mulling and musing
Within his confusion until
"Bingo!" he put all the pieces
Into place and is about to join
The Human Race.

It's Their Problem

Well, isn't that too bad?
My friends just can't understand
Why I am asserting my
God given choices and
They no longer recognize me.
It's their problem to rearrange
Their attitude and accept
What is happening to me.
I won't back down when they
Raise their eyebrows at my
Shift in awareness for it takes
A kind of adjustment to make
Their own mental alterations.

December 2, 1989

All his life words have been his forté,
Set up in columns and neatly spaced
Under precise control with typeface.
They were locked into press forms
In long rows like a prison.
He labored with proportions and size,
Delivering them according to rules
For fixed fees in the advertising world.
His mind ran in circles of accommodations
To demands shouted by surrounding voices,
Until one day he simply turned
On his heel and walked away,
No longer needing the display.
But somewhere in his inner being
He is still promoting something,
He knows not what.

Living Benediction

Over time,
Searching for the right type
Created a maze of instructions
That were getting somewhere,
Only God knew where.
His mind kept being distracted
By outer duties that taxed
His patience and energy.
It was a merry-go-round of illusions
That created a great fog of confusion.
Questions kept popping up
As to what life was all about,
When all he could see was misery.
He didn't know his life events
Were mirrors of his own thinking and
If he could change his thoughts
His life would become
A living benediction.

December 3, 1989

To bring me joy
Just say I love you.
To give me love
Just be there for me.
To lift my spirits
Just smile with your eyes.
To hold my interest
Just absorb me
In your presence.

Counting Stars

Let's throw away our furniture,
Dishes, linen, and bric-a-brac,
Along with our houses,
So we can casually sit and gaze
Into one another's eyes and hearts
Without heavy worldly possessions
Claiming our frequent attention.
Let's be free of gross materiality
So we can have time
To count the stars and listen
To the magic of the Spheres.

December 4, 1989

After we have told all our remembrances
Of intervening years of our friendship,
What will we do to keep up our interest?
We can't feast forever on yesteryears;
We must build upon the present days,
Bringing pleasure and joy from newfound
Ways of being different, searching to
Come together in playful, meaningful ways.
Getting to know each other's eccentricities
Can fill hours with lessons of delight,
Even causing consternation at times
When we hit a snag of discontent.
Will we always smile at each other's jokes?
Or wish at times we could run back
To another time and space for solitude?
Will the walls start to close around us
When the pressure grows inside?
Will love cure all the blues,
Until there is nothing but pink?

December 6, 1989

He said he would be honored
To share my boudoir.
Now that is a real
Vibrant statement that
Left me for a moment
Unhinged.
But then I suppose it was
Within the context of his character
To reach such a foregone conclusion.
After all, we both know
What the other one knows and
Why play games when we both
Know how to score?

December 7, 1989

With open palm I greet you, my friend,
Nothing hidden and nothing to defend,
Just my open heart to feel your pain.
With a divine connection
I hold you close
In my compassionate embrace,
Allowing all the agony to flow away
While you go back to childish love
That should have been your inheritance.
And once again you find your wholeness,
Bringing unity, conviction, and harmony
To express your unique divinity.

December 8, 1989

Can we accommodate
Each other's wholeness?
Standing independent of each other,
But true to our separate identities?
Can we have freedom to be ourselves,
Dreaming our own dreams
Without interference?
Is it possible to have
"At-one-ment,"
Still being needed
And needing each other?
I have my own power
In every part of me,
I can feel and touch and love,
But it's still empty and lonely
Without you beside me.

December 9, 1989

All the words and thoughts
Have come tumbling out
Over months of long
Telephone conversations,
Until there is nothing
More to be said.
Just waiting for eyes
And hands and legs to meet
To take the senses to
Ultimate heights if the
Bodies can still navigate
To match their rhythms
And scintillate together.
The days are quickly passing
When the debating will stop and
We will have to contend
With closer intimate movements
That may prove to be our undoing.

December 10, 1989

Must I give up parts of me
To be loved by you, or will
You accommodate my foibles
Until you scream in protest,
"You're taking more than I get?"
Relationships grow and thrive
By finding ways each can agree
To be themselves and yet remain
United by giving in when needed.
Will you stay put and content
When I run off to another zone,
Or will you wander off to Chicago
While I dawdle at playing alone?
Both need to explore our inner selves
While still trying to ignite a mutual fire.
So let's remember to be close but
Separate in some of our
Accommodations.

Resolutions

Every relationship is a trade-off
Of pluses and minuses, having parts of
Yourself complimented or challenged,
While issues, illusions, and ideologies
Sometimes clash and crumble
In the attempt at resolution.

Mystery Object

Last night he called with bated breath,
Acknowledging receipt of my Christmas gift,
Discovering its shocking implication,
And its very erotic suggestion.
Looking over his shoulder he wondered
If perchance a lurking spirit might be
Watching his furtive glance,
While his heart began to thump at
The mere prospect of what this shiny
Object was saying to his heart.
How could such a piece of metal imply
Without a word what his future holds?
If we live by myths and symbols,
It must be true our minds deceive us
Into conjuring up events to be unfolded.

December 17, 1989

Yesterday I called him mid-afternoon,
Catching him at his lowest ebb.
I must remember when he is with me
To cradle his head in my lap at
That time of day to get him to smile,
Having a bright and dark side I presume,
Like a tiny infant before its feeding.
I must learn to handle him with care,
Knowing his metabolism
Can be his despair.

Letting Go

Today I let go of being too independent,
Allowing others to hug me when I hurt,
Letting go of never needing anyone,
Asking significant others to pull me up
When I feel stuck or glued or cramped
In a place of old complaints and residue
That act like a vise on the arteries,
That stop the free flow to my heart,
Admitting I need that smile or caring voice
To wake me up to count my many blessings.

My Open Heart

I use words to communicate
My capricious open heart --
Not everyone is so lucky.
Many have barriers built
Around their feelings,
Letting their doubts guard them
From their higher source
And playful spontaneity.
Introspection, as well as
Long hours alone, will lead to
The great discovery
That all of humanity,
While full of vanity,
Is seeking its way
Back Home.

December 18, 1989

Needing and wanting you to care
Is such a disturbing feeling.
It scares me to think of
How much I have learned just
Listening to you on the phone
That when I stand waiting
With you in full view,
I'll probably act
Like a real cuckoo!

December 19, 1989

I shall have to wait until
January 10 to open the
Christmas present of you.
Anticipating the warmth
Of your arms and the light
In your eyes to ignite me,
You will be my belated gift.
I promise to be gentle when
Opening up your heart so
Promise me you will be extra
Careful when you unwrap me.
When you unfold my essence,
Handle me gently for I am fragile.
Kiss my heart with sweet embraces,
Hold my spirit kindly while you
Drink from my overflowing cup,
Just enough to quench your thirst.
Then I will catch your merry twinkle
In my open hands and listen
To your heart as it expands.

December 22, 1989

Without the spark of your wit and charm
I could not have gone the long last mile.
You have sustained my walk on that bridge
Until I could be in your arms once again.
Without the daily telepathic messages
To soothe my ever-changing turbulence,
The in-between times of my fluctuating grief,
I could have shriveled into powdery dust.
But your firm grasp on a future dream
Came to my rescue, and brought activity.
My mind comprehended what was intended
While the weeks stretched to months
Until we arrived at a cozy convention
Of blending ourselves
Into a working connection.

Full Circle

Distant lands have lost their glamor
Since I fell in love with you.
All I want is to be anywhere with you.
Exotic destinations do not entice me
When it's more dramatic in your arms.
Never will I need snowy mountains
When I can find exhilaration with you.
Loving you keeps me from wandering,
For all my searching around the globe
Has led me back full circle to you.

December 26, 1989

I need your essence to warm me.
I need your smile to fill me.
I need your voice to thrill me.
I need your heart to guide me.
I need your soul to enfold me.
These gifts from your holy center
Are the only worthwhile jewels
I shall ever desire from you.
In return I will love you forever,
Knowing I need to be needed by you.
All the paths of my life's journey
Were leading back to you and
I wonder how in some part of me
I knew that through the troubled waters
And stormy weather there would be
A warm shelter in your heart for me.
Instincts must be hidden
Within us like a compass
That guides us to each other,
Always bringing us back to love.

December 27, 1989

Let's make-believe we are betrothed
Just to keep the tongues from wagging.
We shall let our hearts take over in
The drama of this unique meeting
As we begin to unite and ignite into
Our own fascinating experiment,
Picking up the pieces of our youth,
Making the jigsaw puzzle of our lives
Create a special mosaic of our destiny.
This is the inevitable year as the
Astral influences congregate,
Making clear how fortune has smiled,
Bringing us back together full circle.
Did our thoughts create this meeting
Or were our hearts always entwined,
Waiting for the appointed time?
Perhaps before we entered this life
We planned to briefly meet and touch
Before our Karma dictated we must fulfill
Separate requirements before we
Could claim each other with the freedom
To be what was intended from the beginning.
Now we have completed all our contracts,
Returning to each other's loving embraces,
Knowing that the first encounter was needed
To complete this prophetic late engagement.

January 1, 1990

When she was a rosebud closed tightly
In her young virtuous chastity,
He fondled her sweet innocent flower,
Intoxicated by her hidden powers,
Starting to show sensuality.
As her petals unfolded with probing
He waited and watched with excitement,
Persisting patiently in his discoveries,
Awakening shyly to his own manhood.
Before he could know her full bloom,
Destiny changed his life course,
Leaving him without a trace
Of the rosebud's sweet smelling perfume.
Now, a half century later, he views
The same antique rose still blooming,
Luring him on by his recurring dreams
Of fondling her faded blossoms,
Still loving the exotic perfume that
Only the full-blown rose can reveal.

January 4, 1990

We live in the now.
We conceived yesterday
As a possibility
For the future.
All space and time
Become a catalyst
To measure our days
Together in eternity.
Hold lightly but firmly
To the moments
So we can become
Encapsulated in
Our loving rapture.

January 5, 1990

Yesterday he lost his furry hat
While shopping in Chicago's Loop,
Which to me is quite an omen
In more ways than one.
First of all his mind was elsewhere,
Being distracted by his newly
Purchased black shiny shoes
That raised his spirits above
The mundane surroundings into
The thought that next week would
Find him in a warmer climate.
So the loss of his hat and head
Did not perturb him greatly,
Knowing that somehow he would
Never need another hat like that
Where his Love was
Waiting in California.

January 7, 1990

Just three more days
Before he arrives and
The butterflies in my
Stomach are beginning
To flutter and rise
In a kind of anticipation
Of what and how and when
Everything will come together again,
Keeping the outer shell whole
While fireworks are buried
Deep inside the mysterious
Dark place of my soul.
Waiting for blast-off time
In my prim orderly life,
Is like waiting for a
Spring flower to open.
One must be patient with time,
For it moves slowly but surely
At nature's own systematic pace,
That defies detection by
Humanity's eyes of what
God in his wisdom
Has in mind.

January 8, 1990

Johnny-Come-Lately is on his way,
Boarding the shiny Amtrak today,
Making a commitment by
Going back to his future,
Taking a second look
A half century later.
He will observe the lovely
City of Angels much tarnished
By homeless junkies and smog
Erupting over past years.
The sleepy-paced rhythm of yore
Has vanished into oblivion
As the anxious politicians
Fight for clean air,
And the silent spirit within
Waits patiently
To be discovered.

January 9, 1990

Today marks the Eve of Rollin.
Tomorrow is like Christmas for me.
Will my heart jump out of my body
As I feel your arms encircle me?
Will your heart be pounding too
As I hold you closely in my arms?
Will we both collapse on the platform
Or will we cover up all the internal stuff
So nobody suspects we have caught on fire?

Balancing Act

He is having his quiet cool down time
While speeding along the railroad tracks,
Getting closer and closer to blasting off.
I hope his blood pressure stays normal
As he tries to eat and sleep to the
Crazy rhythm of the swaying train.
Equilibrium can be affected
By anticipated ecstasy
So I hope he finds his balance by
The time he gets off the train.

The Relevant Question

Will we reciprocate or equivocate?
That is the relevant question.
Can we interact and exchange
Ideas to create a perfect harmony?
Will he spark my humor and wit
With his droll and whimsical side?
Or will I upset and annoy him
Until he annihilates my connection?

Photographs

Jerri Brillhart, Glendale, CA, 1936-37

Rollin Perry, Proofreader at *Esquire Magazine,* Chicago, Illinois, 1935

His daughter-in-law, Connie Perry writes, "It seems he'd rather be the photographer than the subject of photos."

Rollin, San Antonio, Texas, 1991

Jerri on holiday, Hawaii, 1992

Rollin and Jerri, San Antonio, Texas, 1991

January 25, 1990

With his little boy whimsy
He keeps me entertained
By the look in his eye and
The feel of his embrace.
He makes me a prisoner
Of his charms
While entwined in his arms;
My heart thumps with joy
Trying to catch the Express
Of his train as he wonders if
He can stay on board.
As day merges into night
The magic of him envelops me,
Leaving me a captive of love.
It has to be a kind of hypnotism
That makes me a slave of love,
Not caring where I am or
What I do, just pleasing his fancy
As he reels along his path,
Zooming into space,
Watching all his inhibitions
Vanish into thin air.
Will the voyage into each other
Blind our senses to the consequences
That we have lost ourselves
In a dream?

January 26, 1990

He fumbles for his cigarettes.
They're nowhere in sight.
When the urge gets overwhelming
He reaches for her warmth,
Pursing his yearning lips
In the sensuous folds of her.
Oh, he is giving up tobacco
For a far sweeter taste, while
The smoke of love drifts around him
Sending him into outer space.

January 28, 1990

Let's be friends first of all,
Letting everything fall into place.
The kind of pals who walk together,
No one first or last, just watching,
Feeling, hoping, wanting what is best
For each other through the day and night,
Letting the breath rise and fall in
A rhythmic kind of way while
Each heart beats in harmony.
Just let our spirits dictate a
Perfect sense of magic that
Brings a creative flow.

February 5, 1990

I am open to change of every kind,
Knowing that growth comes only
To those who accept and embrace
New challenges that enlarge
Horizons and bring fulfillment
Of one's eternal potential.

February 6, 1990

He demonstrated the use of his will,
Employing a technique called hypnotism.
How simply it was done remains
Such a mystery that he can't believe
His head is screwed on right,
Or if his mind has lost its anchor
To a 60-year-old pattern of habits.
How can one explain a materialization
That defies detection of all illusions?

Aging Embers

As their bodies entwine with
Determination
They practice patterns of
Co-habitation,
Thinking their heart's desire is
Enough
To kindle the heat to a consuming
Fire.
But aging embers ignite very
Slowly,
Needing to be coaxed by a subtle
Kind
Of higher permission from a
Silent
Hidden source in each other's
Soul
That balances all the ingrained
Issues
Called attitudes of morals and
Integrity.
Seeking security in each other's
Bodies
Gives the final sanctity to
Scale
Hidden walls of lifetime
Behavior
Our modern ways have nullified as
Irrelevant.

February 18, 1990

Starting out slowly with caresses,
Like gentle summer breezes
That begin to make you ascend
Easily into a tropical heat,
Making the body lose itself
In a certain timeless rhythm,
While the breath comes faster
The body contorts itself
Into fantastic movements
That plunge you into the
Oblivion of climax.

March 23, 1990

He has gone back home to Illinois, just as he did over 50 years ago. Now that I am older I understand that life for us was different from the start.

Each of us had some karma we came to finish that allowed us to touch each other briefly and travel on to fulfill our destiny. We had different prejudices about life and each had to resolve them. We had subconscious fears in how this was to be accomplished. We had similar problems in life to solve. We used different ways of evolving.

We each arrived at our own solution in our own way in our own time. Dreams have a way of turning out in different ways, but still accomplish the same purpose of softening the heart.

April 8, 1990

As the body is slow to heal, so the mind is slow to change and we must be patient with ourselves, forgiving our error and our ignorance of self-abuse. Would we knowingly inflict pain on ourselves?

It is through trial and error that we have lived and survived for over seven decades. This learning and growing and adapting to change has given us the values we live by. If there is something wrong in our thinking, our bodies will eventually demonstrate the error. Our belief system will be revealed in our lives and our bodies, for good or bad. All pain is a warning sign that we need to change something and we must do the work ourselves because it is an inside job.

We may have others point the way or help us over the rough spots, but eventually we must row our own boat or remain emotionally crippled. To face our own shortcomings is hard work but in order to be more healthy and happy we must take up the challenge and move along our chosen path.

April 11, 1990

Let us depart from illness today,
Boarding the train with unwanted
Woes, accumulated over years of
Hoarding old hurts and memories,
Departing from the station with old
Baggage of regrets, sorrows and losses,
Taking time to dump old problems,
Perceptions and judgments along the
Highway of lost hopes so that
Arriving at our new destination
We will come into our new selves,
Right on time with health,
Happiness and love that will
Bless our homecoming with
Intuition and open arms.

April 18, 1990

So many kinds of doors in life.
Some are open, some are shut and
Some simply get stuck.
The secret is when to open them
Or learn to keep them closed.
But curiosity is strong,
Leading us to peek and pry
Until to our amazement we find
That doors once stuck, now open wide.
The open door can lead us forward
Into an inner space
Where we can get
A much better view
Of God's special place.

Dear Rollin,

All my life I have been trying to rescue weak men. It started when I was a child living with a sick father and watching my mother and my grandmother struggle with this same issue. The whole family was aware of my father's sickness and all attention was centered on his health. He came first, always. Always trying to save him from illness and pain.

I learned strategies of psychological maneuvering, watching, studying, hoping to heal and save people from their own ignorance. My whole life has been one of searching for the truth, for cures and answers to other people's misery, wanting to be the savior of others because I always had more insight and understanding, believing that all ills could be cured -- if only this or that were done.

Believe me, this battle of the Ego against the Soul is a lifetime (or many lifetimes) struggle. This job is God's work and I must stop playing God. If a person gets more attention by being weak and sick and getting everyone to help him, give him sympathy, etc., he must wake up to the con game he is playing. Each chooses his thoughts daily and acts upon them. Each chooses to grow or remain the same. When a person gets sick enough of their old ego patterns they will make the necessary changes, but not until they really want to. I can only be a "Way Shower." I refuse to carry anyone when their stubborn ego refuses to change. Everyone must save themselves.

I am looking for strength and integrity and wholeness in a relationship and I will not tolerate placing myself in the position of thinking I must do the saving. I am sorry but I can no longer condone or help you and please do not keep pleading with me to save you. If you are worth saving, you have to do your own saving until you reach your communication with your own God Self.

Love, Jerri

April 25, 1990

Forgive, forgive, forgive. . .
What is there to forgive?
Weakness in another is just an
Indication that they are still
Stuck at the first grade level,
Trying to learn enough to move on
To the second grade.
There is nothing to forgive.
They are in the state of becoming.
Our irritation is not with them but
With ourselves and our inability to
Accept that they are very slow learners.
The darkness in them is just slow
To be impregnated with the light.
Hold to the image of perfection in them,
Giving them strength to rise with the light.
I must forgive myself for my impatience,
Knowing in some areas
I am a slow learner too.

April 29, 1990

He keeps trying
To beat down my wings
So I will flutter at his will.
He keeps wanting to keep me
In his gilded cage of love,
Cramping and confining me
In a place of constriction,
Near and right there for him.
I need my independence to
Listen to my Muse when I please.
This kind of living seems
To many strange and selfish
But for me it's the heaven I earned.
So let me sit when I want to sit,
Walk when I feel like walking, or
Lie in my bed alone if necessary.

May 3, 1990

In my mind, I hear you saying:
"My woman friend is so provocative,
At times so appetizing and alluring;
She excites my feelings and desires
With her antics and her answers
To unspoken questions that arise in me.
But when I need to control her,
She slips through my senses, aggravating
With her evasive and irritating manner
That antagonizes and vexes me so!
Oh, why are women such
Annoying creatures,
Having unseen powers
To provoke men's emotions
Like spiders that capture them
In webs of devotions?"

May 12, 1990

The rapture and radiance I felt
When you held me ever so gently,
Kissing me in all my open crevices,
Finding our unity deep within.
It was during those moments
Of pleasure I felt at home with you,
But I know in my heart
I also need the freedom
To be alone and whole,
Filled with ecstasy
Miles away from you.

Love Is

Being free to say anything
That springs from the soul,
For in our heart of hearts
There beats a certain kind of
Syncopation with the Source.

Harmonizing

Allow me the pleasure of loving you,
Just the way I find you in every kind of mood.
Allow me to sit in awe and wonder at the
Unique embodiment that you are.
For with all your faults and virtues,
The chemistry of you stirs me into laughter
That reaches my heart and harmonizes me.
We reminisce about past lessons,
Wondering why we never saw the splendor
All around us or heard the internal flow
Of harmony encircling us,
Or understood the beauty
Of an ordinary day when our bodies
Longed for intimacies beyond our grasp,
When life was taken for granted
Until we noticed little by little
The glory and radiance have passed.

He Still Calls

He still calls in the dark hours,
Reaching out with his anxieties
So I can smooth his fevered brow,
Like a good mother kissing away
The daily bruises and hurts.
He needs me to mirror his worth,
To soothe the piled up pain
And years of mistreatment
He brought upon himself by lying
About his needs and wants,
Covering up with aloofness
That starved his spirit,
Alienating him
In his self-inflicted prison.
Can I say the magic words
Of transformation
That will free him
To be himself?

May 17, 1990

Love is the redeeming quality
That lifts our ebbing spirits,
Renewing body, mind and soul,
Giving us the invisible strength
To meet every change of life.
If we have erred in perception
Our bodies will reveal ignorance.
If we fail to find happiness
Love will give us guidance.
If we find ourselves in debt
Love will supply our abundance.
Love is the invisible thread
That holds us in a state
Of wholeness and strength.

October 29, 1990

The warm glow of my peaceful heart
Ignites my being with happiness,
Sending my mind into a place
Of unfathomable heights,
Making me soar to another dimension,
Creating a rhythm of completion.
As I visualize you whole and well,
Embracing me at some appointed hour
With joy, happiness, and thanksgiving,
Bringing us together at long last,
Knowing that there is nothing more
That can separate us from our good
As we expand into the possibilities of
New worlds within us to explore.

November 8, 1990

Like drifting sand,
Like a rolling stone,
My mind tried to find repose,
Weighing all material issues
While my heart kept
Hammering on my brain
To thaw my frozen mass
And let love claim the victory.

Through weeks of vacillation
And capricious wanderings
In erratic journeys while
Adrift in solitary confinement,
I searched for meaning in my life.

At last there came an awareness
That loving you was necessary
To stabilize both of us in
The unfolding of each other,
Swaying peacefully to the
Rhythm of our pendulums.

November 17, 1990

Oh, he is getting better and better,
Bit by bit the pieces of the puzzle
Begin to mesh, starting to syncopate
Until he is better than new with the
Awakening awareness and acceptance
Of the truth of his inner power.
He has time and intelligence to
Comprehend the duality within
That held him shackled to his unreality
While a part of his uniqueness
Was lost somewhere in space and time,
Hidden from his senses, deeper than deep.
But now he is becoming better than new,
Expanding and escaping his own cocoon
To try his wings in his next flight,
Leaving his creeping, crawling chrysalis
While he soars to new heights.

December 13, 1990

He wants to change her name,
Her address, her attitudes
And her bank account.
He wants to possess
Her body, her attention,
Her life and her mind,
Never believing
That is not what
She had in mind.

April 7, 1991

Does youth hold all the treasures
Of love, lust and languish?
Is zest only in younger cells?
Or can it be true that in old age
There are still torrents of splendor
That can arise to amorous occasions,
Stirring a sensitive celibate's heart?
Is it only in the vibrant body
Or just really in the mind
That the heart always yearns
To be attached and loved?
Perhaps satisfaction really comes
In knowing time is running out and
Love must find a way
To contemplate
The wonder of it all.

April 22, 1991

As I behold your radiance,
And bask in your light,
I am thankful for our blessings.
As I become aware of your worth,
Standing close enough to touch,
I am thankful for our blessings.
As thoughts of love surround us,
Keeping us warm and tight,
I am thankful for our blessings.
As we fill our hearts with joy,
Making our days a heaven on earth,
I am thankful for our blessings.

Synchronicity

Will you be there
When I am down?
Will you help me
When I fall below
The standards you
Have set for me?
Will I still want you
When you can't see
Everything my way?
Will I let you win
When my heart says no?
Will our Wills create
A new synchronicity
That keeps us balanced?

May 5, 1991

I straddle the fence,
Moving to and fro.
Shall I simply jump
Or sit contemplating,
And not allow anyone
To push, shove, or kick,
As my Will holds me
In a balancing act,
First this way then that,
While my heart is trying
Desperately to change
The status quo.

May 14, 1991

I shall board the American bird
Winging its way to San Antonio
Where I will rendezvous by the river
With my persistent old Beau
From Chicago of long, long ago.
As we bring each other comfort,
Remembering with seasoned hearts
The innocence once known.
Sharing those reveries of long ago,
We shall rekindle the old flame
Once pure and full of dreams.

May 22, 1991

The pressure is building each day
As the hours just drag in May.
But when June comes
So does the fun
Under the heat
Of the Texas sun,
As we rendezvous
In San Antonio.
Will I slip away and hide or
Will he sleep away
On his side?

May 23, 1991

What caused me to write to you?
What caused you to telephone me?
Were we seeking change by reaching out,
Attempting to hold each other again
To reclaim our long vanished youth?
Did the attraction ever cease
While we grew gray and wrinkled?
During five decades of separation
Were our hearts quietly waiting
For a second chance to complete
Our unfinished love story?

May 24, 1991

It's sunny May
And flowers grow
In me today,
Bursting into love
Under Texas skies.
Will he tell me the truth
When he sits by my side,
Warm and open to the heat
Enveloping us both?
June's moon is so full
While aging hearts melt
At the midnight hour.

May 28, 1991

You can be Editor-in-Chief
While I muse and grow,
Allowing thoughts to escape
My active imagination.
You can cut and paste,
Pondering the type and size
To place upon the page.
I will allow criticism
When it comes to the kind of font
But please allow me space
To find the time to rhyme.
Let's dissolve, destroy, and delete
All fears from our busy minds,
With the purpose of bringing
Faith into our every thought
Until we create and complete
All those wonderful dreams,
Filling our futures with blessings,
Creating constant awareness of
The ever present Divine Flow.
You can be Editor-in-Chief
While I just muse and grow,
Allowing my thoughts to escape
My active childlike imagination.
You can cut, paste, and manipulate
The type and size to place on the page.
I'll allow your experienced criticism
When it comes to font and effect,
But please allow me the time
To conjure up my own rhyme.

June 2, 1991

Has he been in a cage
Just looking at the world
Instead of getting out and
Really seeing life.
Why has he chosen
To hide in safer quarters
Instead of staying in touch
With all the wonderful stuff?

Anxiety is the culprit,
Anchored in that hidden space,
Filling his thoughts with terror
Of being out of control.

In a cage there is safety
If only to shut the door
On other faces of the world.
When faith replaces fear
There will be freedom
To chose isolation
So he can discover
Inner growth.

July 21, 1991

Like an old tiger, he walks slowly, reluctantly, as though he wishes his life to be over. His breath is shallow and at times difficult. His face shows strain and resignation, along with a hidden irritation with people, new ideas, strange food, sounds, and places.

He is trapped in an aging body in a state of disuse. He is irritated with himself and the mask he wears to cover up his feelings. Any enthusiasm for his future is held in check by his logical mind, so that what appears to be true is an illusion. To open his heart would be an act of courage. He would have to give himself permission to awaken to beauty and joy.

He has been a servant of duty. He has served mother and wife during their declining years. He has been sensitive to their needs at the expense of his own, and lived a life devoid of human tenderness. He is sensitive to other people's pain while obsessed with his own safety. He is like a ship without a rudder, moving endlessly through the motions of life without a map or a destination. He is starved for love and yearns for it, but he believes others will only hurt him.

The record keeps spinning in the same groove of his belief that people are something to be feared and not enjoyed. He has lived the outer life of obedience to God's Golden Rule but in the innermost recesses of his mind, he has not understood the life of the Spirit.

I Cannot Marry You My Dear

I cannot marry you my dear,
For loving you would enslave
My Spirit to your needs,
Your wants and your kisses.
It would smother my soul,
With your constant chatter
And my observations of your
Aging body and its adjustments,
Driving me crazy with your demands
To love you when your mood is low,
Seeking my balance and vibrations,
Needing my motherly ministrations,
That would suck the marrow from my bones.
You call it love and need and desire,
Trying to forget your emptiness,
Knowing you reach for my fire
To warm your ego-centered heart.
My left hand shows no jewels,
No symbols of vowed promises,
No signs of any encumbrances.
Jewels once shown on my finger
Spoke of binding words of love.
Now I stretch my hand in freedom,
Wondering if I will ever again commit
Myself to jewels that bind like promises.

August 4, 1991

Did I spurn your love?
Did I hurt your ego?
Did I step on your feelings?
Did I upset your dogmas?
Sorry, sorry, sorry, dear.
It is in our attitudes that we differ;
Each uses his unique perceptions,
Seeing what experience has taught,
Be it narrow, rigid, or negative,
Be it wide, open, or optimistic.
I let you go to your Comfort Zone,
Believing what your attitudes dictate,
Allowing you to grow in new dimensions,
While I keep growing into mine.

September 26, 1991

We are all magicians
Creating our own illusions,
Fascinated by our lives
Shaped by our contrivances,
Each holding an air of mystery
Within our secret hearts.
Some play at being perfect,
While others dance with joy,
But I am always pondering
Which mountain I might climb.
So I sit in contemplation
With all my pros and cons
Willing everything to change
In my very fickle heart.

October 4, 1991

In my heart of hearts
I am free to see my dream,
Holding in my mind
The seed of thought,
Waiting for the blossoming
Of the passion fruit,
While in thought I
Water the tiny seed,
Visualizing fulfillment
Every hour I embrace
Beauty, joy, and happiness,
Contemplating its completion,
Beholding the astonishment
In your eyes when you realize
The ecstasy of our love.
We will be beside ourselves
With the rapture,
Savoring the glory
Of our winter love.

February 14, 1992

When that pound of Godiva miniature chocolates arrived two weeks late for my birthday last year, I was shocked at his extravagance, but secretly I knew I deserved them. I loved his gesture of generosity but it was rather an insult after our long friendship was drawing to a close. I felt it in my bones, I knew it in my heart, and somehow I was glad it was coming to an end. It was like a subtle closing of a door.

I kept the chocolates out of sight for about six weeks because they were not what my doctor advised at my age. Once opened, the temptation would be there to help sweeten my life when I felt unloved, old, and out of touch with the world around me.

It had been so easy for him to make a phone call and give his Visa number sending the chocolates to California. It took about five minutes of his time and interest. There was no birthday card this time either. It was a gift long overdue and I felt it was his deliberate way of saying, "Let's forget about what we said to each other in our separate desperations. Growing old is difficult enough without having unrequited love to stress us out."

Finally, I brought out the box of Godiva chocolates at Thanksgiving after my guests had finished the turkey feast. The eyebrows on my daughter's face arched high in surprise. All she said was, "Oh, he sent you chocolates again!" I smiled a very small smile that looked well on my 75-year-old face and nothing more was said.

Well, today I finished the last piece of Godiva chocolates. It is like a farewell gesture to my first romantic encounter with him when I was 17. He had hoped, after six months of long distance phone calls from Chicago and a two-month visit with me in California, that I would finally say "yes" to his constant request to "Marry me, marry me."

After all these years both our spouses had died within six months of each other and he thought we could rekindle our long lost love and end our days together. However, my heart could not be aroused to see it his way.

At this stage of my life, I am not ready to give him the necessary sustenance he expected of me to feed his ego, his depression, and his ill health. He was unable to keep up with my active, curious, growing personality. He is set in a mold of complacency, as his body grows rigid due to lack of movement. His chronological age determines his conduct but he is asleep to the possibilities of his spirit.

We are years apart biologically and psychologically, but only two years apart in real age. As a result of these differences, there would always be a constant friction that would create enough stress to finish us both off in a short time. It is far better to remember what used to be, while savoring Godiva chocolates.

P.S. The Godiva chocolates were really Fannie May chocolates.

A Marriage Should Be An Adventure

Marriage is a challenge. You give up your personal simplicity to participate in a relationship. It means yielding time and again. That's why it is a sacrament. It becomes life building, life fostering and an enriching experience -- not an impoverishment -- because you are giving to somebody else. Marriage is helping each other to develop and bloom, to be something astonishing and unexpected.

No matter who you tie your life to, you're going to find the person mysterious. The sexes are deeply mysterious to each other. There will be a lot that you didn't know about the person, things even the person himself didn't know. Remember, the person is having the same problem in relation to you. Both are changing all the time.

So often we want to freeze the other person into a position. Naturally people have a notion of what marriage ought to be and the marriage they want. You can't have that and have the adventure of a loving marriage. It's got to be one or the other.

Wherever love takes you, there you are, and that's the adventure!

CPSIA information can be obtained
at www.ICGtesting.com
Printed in the USA
FSHW010027210219

9 780991 197057